D0912612

Daddy Doesn't Want Me

by

Rick Manis

Empyrion Publishing
Winter Garden FL
EmpyrionPublishing.com

Empyrion Publishing
PO Box 784327
Winter Garden, FL
info@EmpyrionPublishing.com

Unless otherwise noted, all Scripture quotations are from the King James Version of the Bible.

Other versions are acknowledged as follows:

NAS – New American Standard
NLT – New Living Translation
CEV – Contemporary English Version
NIV – New International Version

Printed in the United States of America

Table of Contents

Forward

The approaching of Father's Day is the inspiration for this writing. The holiday will bring beaming accolades from sons and daughters about how their dad is the greatest man in the world. I will hear and read testaments to strength, stability, courage, and wisdom.

My relationship with my dad wasn't so rosy. In fact, it was very messy. There are more of these stories than one might think.

Everyone's story is unique. Nobody is perfect according to human standards, so we all have our own individual experiences in the complex father/child dynamic. However, I feel that mine is one that should be told. While it is very relatable to the many who did not have such a good relationship with their earthly father, the worth of my story is in its redemption.

In these pages can be found hope, peace, and joy. It is the story of something that is bigger and more powerful than our hurts, our mistakes, and our dysfunctions

This is a story of unconditional love. I call it "Daddy Doesn't Want Me".

My Dad, My Hero

Chapter 1

Dad was my hero. He was the smartest man in the world in my young eyes, and I felt lucky to have him for my dad. He was without a doubt my very favorite person in the whole world, even though I never felt that I was his favorite. I felt that he liked my siblings more. Maybe he didn't. It didn't change the fact that he was *my* favorite.

I would get happy when he came home from work. I often had something to show him, or I might ask him to do something with me. He usually put me off, letting me know that he didn't have time.

To be fair, there were moments he would make some time for me, but they were few enough and special enough that I probably remember each one of those times. He wasn't a grouch at all, but he was an old-fashioned dad who believed that his love was proven by providing food and shelter for us.

Being old-school, Dad believed it was more important to eliminate the bad, rather than accentuate the good. I remember asking him why he never seemed to notice any of the good I did.

His answer was, one hole in the pants ruins the whole thing.

I vividly recall twice in my life that he said he was proud of me, once while I was playing baseball. He only attended a few games over the years that I played, and I remember often criticisms. The other time was when I heard him talking to some friends of his about how smart he thought I was. I don't think he ever said that to me.

By moral standards, Dad was a good man, an honest man who never took a penny that wasn't his. He was good with his hands. It seemed he could figure out how to do or build anything. He worked on the space program at Cape Kennedy, which made me even more proud to call him my dad.

Dad and Mom got divorced when I was twelve years old. They let us choose who we would rather live with. I wanted to be with my hero. I couldn't imagine being away from him, so Dad was my choice.

He had a tough job, keeping me, my sister, and brother by himself. Dad worked during the day, and he was always concerned that we were okay while he was gone. He set restrictive rules on us to keep us close to the house.

I was always a free spirit by nature, sometimes skipping school and breaking his rules often. This was a great source of stress to Dad.

We lived with our single dad for a year before he married again. We liked his wife and her two sons well enough, and we had the idea that the merging of our families would be similar to "The Brady Bunch" TV show.

My Dad, My Enemy

Chapter 2

When Dad remarried, he bought a four-bedroom home and we began the blending of our families.

There were troubles from the beginning. There were jealousies among us kids and disagreements about fairness. It was hard on Dad's relationship with his wife, and a decision was made to send us to stay with our mom for a month when summer started. At least that's what we were told.

When a month had passed, Mom let me know that we would not be going back to live with Dad. I ran to the phone and called him. He verified that we would now be living with Mom. I cried like a baby. I wanted my dad and now I was a thousand miles away from him.

I held out hope that this was temporary, but eventually he quit taking my calls and I would have no more contact with him for five years.

I felt that my life was crushed. My identity was nothing. I could count on nothing, I was worth nothing. I was so unlovable, that even my dad didn't want me.

During this time, I became a drug-using petty criminal, going in and out of jail. My source of adventure came from hitch-hiking around the country.

My roaming eventually took me back to Florida, where at the age of eighteen, I made contact with Dad. There was still a part of me that wanted his love, his approval. However, this grown son of his was not much that he could approve of. I was a long-haired floater, a stupid drop-out, a law-breaker with no ambition.

We did have some long conversations, and he did inspire me to want more in life. Yet in these conversations, all of my dysfunctions were blamed on my own stupidity. There was no real reconciling. It was little better than tolerance for each other.

Dad was now divorced again, and living alone. He offered to let me and my siblings move in with him. He would help me to get my high school diploma and get into college.

We moved in with Dad, but I was very independent in my mind by that time, and I was used to following my own rules. I found that I couldn't abide with someone so authoritarian. I felt that this man had thrown me away years earlier. In my mind, he didn't care about me during the years that I needed him, so he really had no right to tell me what to do at this time.

His words didn't carry much weight with me, and I continued to be a rebel. Our arguments became so heated at times that it nearly came to blows.

The man who was once my hero had become my hated enemy.

So very early one morning, I stuffed my clothes into a pillow case. I scrambled some eggs and put them in a little Tupperware container. Dad had a pint of Jack Daniel's whiskey in the cupboard. He never touched it, and I had had my eye on it for some time. I stuck it in my pillow case. I grabbed a dollar off of the counter that Dad had left out for my brother's lunch money.

With these provisions, I set out on foot back to Oklahoma. There was nothing great awaiting me there, but at least it was away from my dad.

For the next couple of years there would be more drug and alcohol abuse. I tried college, but dropped out when I was kicked out of the dormitory for rule violations. I hitchhiked around the country from coast to coast. There would be more trouble with the law and more jail time.

Then an amazing thing happened.

Daddy Doesn't Want Me

My Miracle

Chapter 3

In April of 1979, at the age of 21, I received Jesus as my personal savior. It was miraculous! It was a dramatic and radical change in my life. I felt so full of love and life that I was able to quit all of my bad habits.

I loved my salvation and felt so close to God. It was wonderful. The sky seemed bluer and life seemed sweeter. I felt that I was loved by God, and that I loved everybody. My vision of life became clearer. I could see!

This was what I had been looking for all of my life, to be loved and accepted. I began experiencing more joy. I was loved, and I felt more complete.

I became totally involved in church, and I was occasionally preaching from the pulpit in just a couple of years. I attended a Bible college, then became an associate pastor. Eventually, I felt called to build a church in Titusville, Florida, where I had lived for many years as a child.

In 1989, my wife and I, along with our two young daughters moved to Florida to start the church.

Dad lived 30 miles away in Orlando, so we went to visit him. This would be my first contact with Dad in twelve years. The last time we had seen each other we nearly got into a fist fight, but things were different now. I had changed for the better and so much time had passed. I wanted my kids to know their grandpa.

The first visit to Dad's house was very cordial. There was some awkwardness and we spoke to each other like a couple of friendly businessmen. I didn't come with any agenda, other than to show love to my dad. As far as I was concerned, he owed me nothing, and I didn't have any pain from the past that I needed to hash out. I was loved by God and my heart had been healed. I had no demands from this man. I just truly loved him.

I wanted to hug him, but we shook hands (like a couple of businessmen) at the end of the evening and I told him that I loved him. He replied very matter-of-factly that he loved me too.

It wasn't a wonderful reunion, but it was a start.

As time went by, I would spend more and more time with Dad. We became very comfortable together. He saw that my love for him was unconditional, and that our past had no effect on how I felt about him.

I never confronted him about his past decisions that involved me. I was not the needy, dysfunctional child that I once was. I was more whole, more complete, and completely loved by God so I had a more complete love to give to my dad.

We liked to go fishing together, and we had such good times. We were buddies, but more importantly, he was my dad and I was his son. We both became very secure and happy in those roles together.

I do remember a time or two when the past would come up in our conversation. Apparently, he had somehow rewritten it in his mind. He was more heroic in his version of our story than I remember; and I know that he altered it to put himself in a better light. That was fine with me. I wanted Dad to have peace in the later years of his life. I didn't want him to have to wrestle with a burden of guilt or blame from me, so I never corrected his version of the story. I let him remember it the way that he wanted. I loved this man, and he had felt enough pain in his life without me adding any more to it.

Unconditional love is a powerful thing. I personally think it is the most powerful thing in the universe, because unconditional love is God.

Daddy Doesn't Want Me

My Dad, My Ministry Partner

Chapter 4

Dad didn't think very highly of Christianity. He thought most churches were scams and most preachers were dishonest. He used to warn me while I was growing up, to never become too religious. He said it could make me crazy.

However, Dad did consider himself spiritual. He was a smart man who loved to read and study. His belief was a mixture leaning mostly to a universalist new age spirituality. He believed in cultivating psychic mind power, out-of-body travel, and reincarnation among other "things".

So there I was, the son whom he had warned about religion (meaning

Christianity), and I was pastoring a church.

I'm sure he thought I was in excess about some things related to my Christianity (and in hindsight, he may have been right about some of it); but I also know that he liked my wholesome lifestyle, my leadership, and gracious spirit. He would not have ever chosen this life for me, but he knew it was better than the way I was before.

Dad and his wife would visit my church now and then. His wife had actually gotten saved a few years earlier, and it showed. She loved what I was doing. She loved God, and she was proud of me.

Well, the day came when Dad walked the aisle and made a profession of Jesus as his savior. Dad got saved!

I started a second church in Orlando. Dad and his wife started coming faithfully to my church. He was eager to help in any way. Imagine that. Me and my dad were working in the ministry together.

I think Dad became my best evangelist. He was retired, but took a job driving for an airport ride service. He would often tell his passengers about our church, inviting them to attend.

It was shortly afterward, that I quit pastoring, and began my full-time traveling ministry. I moved away to another state, and I would see my dad every few months.

Daddy Doesn't Want Me

My Dad's Final Days

Chapter 5

Dad eventually bought a motor home and traveled all over the country. He stopped by to see me for a few days. He was doing something he always loved doing. I think it was the happiest time of his life. I remember thinking how glad I was that Dad was enjoying himself so much.

Some months after that, Dad called me from his home. He told me that he had lung cancer. It was advanced, and he didn't have much time. He said he was going to begin setting his affairs in order.

I began making plans to visit him, but in just a few days, he died.

I attended his memorial service, and thought about how thankful I was to have known my dad. I was thankful that I wasn't attending the memorial of a biological someone whom I barely remembered or barely understood. I was thankful that I got to know him intimately. I was thankful for all the quality time, and the laughs we shared.

As a child and a teen, I wished for his love and attention. As a man, I got it. I got the best version of him. I loved my dad and he loved me.

"He will restore the hearts of the fathers to their children and the hearts of the children to their fathers..." - Malachi 4:6 NAS

To God be all of the glory. God can do anything. He can change a heart. He can restore bad relationships and make them better than they ever were.

Without Unconditional Love, this story could not be written. I would have lived out my days struggling with a hidden bitterness. I would have continued with a fear of rejection that I didn't understand. It would have impacted my relationships and decisions for the rest of my life.

God is Love. The power of His Unconditional Love is the most beautiful and only perfect thing that there is. When we really know that God loves us, it fulfills us in a way that eradicates our need for anything from anybody. It makes us big. It enables us to give, to love, to bless.

Unconditional Love is the answer for us all. Unconditional Love is God. (I John 4:8).

"May you experience the love of Christ, though it is too great to understand fully. Then you will be made complete with all the fullness of life and power that comes from God." - Ephesians 3:19 NLT

The Lord Will Take You In

Chapter 6

Please know that my story is not intended to require anything of you. There is no pressure on you to reconcile with anyone, or to do anything that I have done.

It is intended to tell the story of a Love that has no requirements. It's a Love that none of us can emulate. It is received as freely as it is given. Yet it does shine out of us after it has first shined within us.

Please know that you are really loved. This is not theology nor theory with me. It is the most real, undeniable experience of my existence.

"For my father and my mother have forsaken me, but the LORD will take me in." – Psalm 27:10 ESV

I think this verse describes the feeling of my relationship with the Creator. It really feels like He has taken me into His care, His home, His counsel, His Love.

He is truly my heavenly Father, again, not in theological theory or symbolism; but in reality, in feeling, in experience.

When you allow yourself to be perfectly loved by the One who is Love, you can no longer feel alone, abandoned, or rejected.

So many of us have been rejected, molested, or abused in other ways. Often, our pain resulted in disfigured self-images, or damaged emotional conditions.

A soul that hungers for Love easily becomes an addictive personality.

Legalistic religion does not offer what will heal our hearts. It only offers a covering mask for our selfish actions.

God loves the addicted, the selfish, the self-destructive, the afraid, the promiscuous, the hateful…

"I will not leave you as orphans; I will come to you." – John 14:18 ESV

God has no condemnation to give, only a pure Love with no conditions.

"Come to me, all of you who are tired from carrying heavy loads, and I will give you rest." – Matthew 11:28 GNT

As you consider the reality of God's Love and care for you, your heart opens up to it.

Believe it. Receive it by faith. Just thank God for it!

As you receive it. Your heart becomes fulfilled. The pain heals. You get a new spring in your step, a new smile on your face, a new song in your heart.

It's so real, and so good, I plead that everyone would drop any other ideas about God, and give His personal Love for you the attention it deserves.

*"One who has unreliable friends soon comes to ruin, **but there is a friend who sticks closer than a brother**."* – Proverbs 18:24 NIV

Enjoy.

About Me

God has been good to me. He has allowed me to speak and teach in thousands of speaking engagements, where I've had the joy of seeing countless lives changed by God's Love.

I like to use personal examples of faith adventures, self-effacing humor, and a general graciousness to encourage people to go ahead and experience the Kingdom of Heaven in this life. My message is that God has given us all we need in Jesus Christ, and if we believe, we can enjoy every bit of it.

I guess I have an ability to relate to all types of people, so I'm invited to many different kinds of groups, churches and organizations.

If you want to come and speak to your group, just drop me a line.

To contact me please write or call:

Rick Manis Ministries
PO Box 784327
Winter Garden FL 34778
863-703-0780

Or visit us on the web at:
Rickmanis.com

Or email us at:
info@rickmanis.com

Other books by Rick Manis:

Fullness! Living Beyond Revivals and Outpourings

The Now Zone

Glory in the Glass

Resurrection! Trusting the God I Knew with a Future I Didn't

Get them at Amazon.com or Rickmanis.com